The 3 C's System

Your One Evening Guide to Health and Wealth Creation

By Tess Tims

The 3 C's System:
Your One Evening Guide to Health and Wealth Creation

All rights reserved
Copyright © 2013 by Tess Tims

Interior Book Design and Layout by
Integrative Ink

ISBN: 978-1-4943949-7-4

No part of this publication may be reproduced, stored in a retrieval system, or transmitted in any form or by any means electronic, mechanical, photocopying, recording, or otherwise, without the written permission of the author or publisher.

Table of Contents

Introduction v
   How Donna Overcame Chaos vi
Chapter 1: Chaos Awareness 1
   My Story of Chaos 2
   5 Tips to Identify the Chaos in Your Life 8
   5 Steps to Prevent Chaos in Your Life 9
   Parting Words about Chaos 20
   The Chaos Awareness Questionnaire 21
Chapter 2: Clarity Awareness 23
   5 Tips on Achieving Clarity Awareness 26
Chapter 3: Commitment Awareness 33
   10 Tips to Help You Stay Committed to Your Goals 33
   Parting Words about Commitment Awareness
   What You Think About, You Bring About 37
Conclusion 39
Acknowledgments 41
About Tess 45

Introduction

Success doesn't have to be complicated, confusing, or drawn out—and neither should the tools you rely on to help you get what you want! Give me an evening of your time, and I will give you the keys to mastering *The 3 C's System: Chaos Awareness, Clarity Awareness, and Commitment Awareness.*

Anyone thinking success has to be a complicated and confusing struggle—even if this has been your experience in the past—is about to discover a new and empowering Truth.

Do you know anyone who lives a chaotic life? Do you know anyone who continuously self-sabotages their life with worry, anxiety, and fear?

Chances are you know several people living a chaotic life: One of those people might be you.

My goal in writing this book is to be an inspiration to you in transforming your way of thinking forever. My *3 C's System* will change your life for the higher good. *The 3 C's System* has definitely changed my life.

Wallace Wattles, author of *The Science of Getting Rich*, said, "Man can form things in his thought, and by impressing his thought upon formless substance, can cause the thing he thinks about to be created." This thinking resonated with me, and I soon learned that when you grow your worth, you grow yourself.

I discovered how to create whatever I want in life, and developed *The 3 C's System*.

Let me show you how to apply this quick, simple, easy-to-understand system to overcome any challenge with which you are faced. First, identify the cause and nature of your Chaos. Second, analyze and get Clarity on your situation. Finally, make a firm Commitment and a plan of action.

How Donna Overcame Chaos

Donna, one of my coaching clients, had a lot of challenges in her life: Her car constantly broke down, her kids kept getting in trouble, and she was losing money in her multi-level marketing business. Soon she had another financial dilemma about attending her company's yearly marketing seminar. She really wanted to attend so that she could network with some of the top sales producers at her company. She knew if she learned a few more strategies from experts, she could turn her business around. Money was tight in her household, and her husband did not share her vision of further investing in her business. When it was time to schedule her trip to the company event, her husband told her bluntly, "You will not take money from our household to fund expenses for a seminar." Donna was devastated. Her husband's words rang in her ears for days. She was confused, upset, and frustrated with her husband. Donna was in a state of Chaos. Here is how she turned it around.

After pondering on several ideas, Donna came up with a solution and reached Clarity Awareness. First, Donna got out of her way and changed her thinking. She could not blame her husband for his words. She could not feel sorry for herself and give up. Donna decided to take charge of her career. She took decisive action and analyzed how she could generate money without disturbing her family's budget. Donna's solution was right in front of her with unique products she could package, market, and sell to some of her best customers. Donna made a commitment to finance her trip to the yearly seminar with the untapped resources she already had. Within 72 hours of Chaos, Donna had all the money she needed to register and travel to the company seminar, plus newfound confidence in knowing how to transform her thoughts of Chaos into Clarity, Commitment, and action toward achieving her dreams. Today, Donna is living her dream as a successful entrepreneur.

Have you ever been in a similar situation where Chaos was overtaking you? Have you ever felt you needed Clarity to make a decision? Perhaps you have felt uncommitted in reaching goals. What is holding you back in your life right now?

This book holds the keys to transforming you from Chaos into Clarity and Commitment toward turning your dreams into reality. This book chronicles the results of what can happen when you become aware of the challenges, mistakes, inconsistencies, and chaos encountered in daily living.

No one likes being in the Chaos of fear, doubt, and worry. Chaos keeps you from accomplishing your goals. It keeps you stuck when you should be racing ahead. For a while, I experienced Chaos in my life through financial stress and thoughts of failure. At one time, it seemed as if I could not make any right decisions in any phase of my life, whether in business, finance, or even personal relationships. My life was in a downward spiral. Ultimately, I committed to having the best in life. I committed to having free time, financial freedom, and excellent health.

Was there ever a time when you realized you were creating the same chaos for yourself, but in a different situation? Chaos always had a way of creeping up on me and holding me back. Whenever I tried to change, it seemed my life was becoming even more chaotic. I floundered and reverted right back to my old habits, or I tried new things that were not well thought out or even self-destructive. Years ago, before I developed *The 3Cs System,* I thought all I needed to live the American dream was to start and operate a successful business. My business was financially successful. I worked long hours, and I began to lose connection with my family and friends. My health began to fail, and there was no time for free time. I was unhappy and in Chaos. Does this situation sound familiar to you? Are you working so hard you don't enjoy life?

A crisis forced me to change my thinking about success. I knew I had to commit to change because my life was falling apart all around me. This is a perfect example of Clarity Awareness. I became aware of my thinking. The power of thought was my key to overcoming chaos, and I had to overcome what's known as "failure thinking." At the time of my crisis, I had a lot of "failure thinking." I had thoughts like, "Why me," "I don't deserve this," "This always happens to me," "I am not pretty enough," "I need to wait, this is not the right time," "I don't have enough money," "I am not smart enough," and "My daughter needs to finish school." My negative thoughts produced negative results, which turned into Chaos, fear, worry, and doubt. Then I noticed I was in a state of Clarity Awareness. I wanted to change my life and made a conscious DECISION to do so, called Commitment Awareness. Then I took action, and things really changed for me.

I started visualizing what I deserved—and wanted—for my life. I transformed into the Commitment Awareness state.

Have you ever had "failure thinking" like mine? Did you know that "failure thinking" causes Chaos in your life? Do you know you can change the Chaos in your life by changing your thinking?

I have the formula for your success in eliminating your Chaos. It's called *The 3 C's System*. Keep reading, and your life will transform to allow you to accomplish all your dreams. Rest easy! I will break down *The 3 C's System* so you can learn and apply it within minutes of finishing this book. You will learn how to recognize:

1. **Chaos Awareness**

2. **Clarity Awareness**

3. **Commitment Awareness**

Chaos Awareness is the first step. Why? Because "Chaos" is traditionally something we consider "bad." Actually, Chaos is often a call to action telling us we need to find Clarity and become committed to an action. Chaos is where many of us find ourselves most of the time if we are not aware of *The 3 C's System*.

It's hard to find success without rising above your Chaos, and in my case, Chaos is exactly what led me to the other *2 C's*. Here is an example of the First C and how it can lead you to success.

Chapter 1
Chaos Awareness

Life is a series of choices. You can choose to be happy or sad; you can even choose to be a failure or success. You are the architect of your destiny. When you refuse to make a choice and allow others to choose for you, you are still making a choice—*to relinquish control*. After weighing all your options, you are always in the best position to make the best choice for you. Choose to live a life free of Chaos.

One definition of Chaos is, "to be out of control." Chaos results from making poor, downright bad, or even NO choices. In other words, you enter into a "hot mess."

What if you were to choose to change the definition of Chaos? In other words, change your thinking about Chaos. That's what I did. In all that I've been through in life—and you're about to find out just *what* I've been through—I choose to believe Chaos doesn't have to be avoided, and it's not all bad. Chaos can be a catalyst for positive change.

Sometimes we need to learn how NOT TO DO a thing in order to learn to do it correctly. Sometimes we need to learn the hard way before we appreciate the easy way. Many times we appreciate a thing more when it's harder to accomplish. Likewise, sometimes we need to experience how we don't want to live in order to realize how we DO want to live. Can you relate to that statement?

Chaos taught me how I didn't want to live, how I didn't want to feel, and how much I wanted to succeed in every aspect of my life. Chaos takes on many forms. For example, a busy restaurant during the lunch rush hour can look disorganized and chaotic. But if that same restaurant is staffed and managed well with friendly, organized personnel, the Chaos is actually controlled activity. Your perception of Chaos determines your definition: Either the restaurant is a complete disaster or it is wildly successful. Your perception tells you whether you are in a restaurant with a bunch of people in tip aprons freaking out!

Only you can tell the difference. To help you understand the meaning of Chaos—the good, the bad, and the ugly of being out of control—let me share my own story in hopes that you can not only learn from my mistakes but also realize that you're not alone if Chaos is what you're experiencing now.

My Story of Chaos

I was raised in an entrepreneurial family. My mother worked as a nanny and housekeeper until she had her fourth child and decided she wanted to improve her life and pave the way for her children's future. Although she had finished high school, she desired a college education. She heard college was demanding and expensive, even for a single person. Yet she was undeterred. With four young children, some still in diapers, she enrolled in college. Her friends and family told her, "Don't do it. Your children are too young. You won't have time to study. You are not smart enough." It appeared she was creating Chaos in her family. Now, in her mid-seventies, she has several advanced degrees and a career doing what she loves. In the process of obtaining her education, she taught her children by example the value of perseverance in the face of unimaginable obstacles. All of her children and grandchildren are college educated. My mother paved the way for her family members to choose their destinies through education.

Before becoming an entrepreneur, my dad worked at a plant earning $1.25 per hour. In the mid-sixties, it was hardly enough money to raise a family of four children with a wife. He was both financially and personally frustrated, so he, too, made a decision that he wanted more for our family. My dad looked around and saw that the successful people in town all owned their own businesses. I was ten years old at the time, and I saw my dad go from making less than minimum wage to owning several successful businesses on the Gulf Coast of Mississippi.

My father owned and operated a motel, mattress factory, a cement company, and a barbershop. He went from earning $2,600 a year to more than $300,000 in the '70s. This was a major accomplishment for a black man in Mississippi—or anywhere else in America.

As my dad's success grew, money wasn't an object but time was scarce. My four siblings and I all worked with my dad in the family businesses. I developed a work ethic by watching my dad. He was a competitive businessman. In a few short years, he had contracts with hotels, hospitals, and universities to manufacture mattresses and mattress covers. Each of my siblings and I learned an aspect of the manufacturing business. By the age of twelve, I knew how to sew and participated with my siblings in an assembly line to turn scrap cloth into mattresses. One brother would make the box spring, one would stuff mattresses with cotton, one would put buttons on the mattress, and then my dad would seal the mattress together. As a child, it was amazing to experience. Learning to sew and use those skills in my dad's company was the impetus for one of my first business ventures: designing clothes for my teenage friends. It was fun.

More than fun, it was constructive. My dad taught us a great work ethic. His leading by example allowed us to understand that we could achieve anything if we took action and worked hard to achieve it.

I thought life was great, with my dad showering us with anything money could buy. I remember my dad worked all the time and seldom had free time. Later in life, I would emulate my dad. I, too, worked long hours. I was a single parent, and like my dad, I had a strong work ethic. It came at a high price until I learned to work smart, not hard.

By the time I was a teenager, my dad's business ventures began to decline. Before I finished high school, my dad had lost all his money and businesses. I could feel turmoil, and I didn't understand it. I now know my dad worked hard, not smart. My father knew how to work and earn money, but he didn't know all of the other important nuggets required to maintain and manage a successful business. I went from wearing $300 boots and diamonds at age twelve to being on welfare in a few short years. It was a traumatic time for my family.

At seventeen years old, I became pregnant, and my father disowned me as if I had committed murder. I was thrown out of the house with no money, no clothes, and no transportation. I was homeless, with what I thought were few options. Soon, I gave birth to my beautiful daughter. She was my bright light in a sea of mayhem. Here I was, a teenage mother on welfare. My situation looked extremely bleak. Out of the chaos, I thought and thought of how I could turn my situation around. Deep down inside, I knew I had to live a better life for me and my daughter. I began to tell myself, "This is not me. This is not who I am." I was really confused and didn't know who I was or how I would survive. After repeating the statement over and over for several weeks, I began to believe in me.

When my daughter turned four weeks old, I marched down to the Department Of Human Services and declared that I wanted to be removed from welfare; I was getting a job, and I was going to college to provide a better life for me and my daughter. I had no idea of how I was going to do it, but I made the commitment. I stayed focused and determined. After six years of part-time study, I received my B.S. degree in Computer Science.

Upon graduation, I landed a career in corporate America, where I worked for several years. Then I had another life altering experience. I was laid off. Again I had no income and few prospects. This time, I had accumulated a car note, mortgage, private schooling for my daughter, and a host of other bills. I was in a state of Chaos. This was the moment when I made the decision never to let corporate America alter my life again. I went back to what I'd learned in childhood: how to create my own income. I took control of my destiny. This was my Chaos Awareness.

Have you ever been in a predicament where you thought there was no hope? Nearly thirty years ago, I was jobless and thought there was no hope. It was a major crisis for me. Like many people in a crisis, I initially had no plan. I had to create a solution. That's when I created Clarity Awareness. I thought about my future and what it was supposed to include. I made a list of the things I wanted and did not want in my life. I refused to consider the obstacles I might face. Then I took action and became committed. I went back to school, learned a new career, and launched a new business. I went from what I thought was the security of a corporate job to the excitement of business ownership. Unknowingly, I entered Chaos again. While I grew up watching my dad run his own business, I had no clue about successfully maintaining a profitable business. I thought all I needed was an income greater than my expenses.

The Chaos caused by my inexperience of business sent my life into a spiral. Whatever I did, whatever new venture I started, there never seemed to be enough. Not enough business, not enough clients, not enough permits, and never enough money. Have you ever been in a similar situation?

Shortly after finishing Beauty College, I opened my first salon. It was fabulous, with mirrors everywhere, marble flooring, and fully stocked with inventory. But it had one big problem: IT HAD NO CLIENTS!

I also didn't have a marketing plan designed to attract new clients. It got so bad I couldn't even pay a $42 water bill. I was trying to outrun Chaos yet again. I analyzed my situation and realized that I had to do something quick. I began to look for opportunities to expand my skills as a way to attract clients.

I didn't know it then, but I was subtly beginning to build my brand. I made certain that I didn't limit my options to my current location. I sought training all over the United States. I enrolled in continuing education classes, which helped me immediately. I went from having a few clients a week to 100 clients a week. I was committed to success. I worked more than twelve hours a day and had a staff of several employees. My dreams were coming true. I thought I had made it. But there was one BIG problem lurking in the background. I had no social life, no time for my beautiful daughter, and I started to have aches and pains everywhere. Have you ever had a time when you realized you were creating one chaotic mess after another? Have you ever wondered how to stop the downward spiral of chaos?

Then I received a call from my great friend Melissa from Beauty College. She invited me to dinner and cocktails. Every week, for months, Melissa called and invited me to a different function, and every week I told her, "I'm sorry, I have to work." She even invited me to a weekend skiing trip in Colorado. My answer was always the same: "I'm sorry, I have to work." Melissa was relentless and never gave up. One day she asked if I worked on weekends, and I replied, "I work every weekend!" She gasped and said, "Tess, you really need to do something different. You need to **work smart** instead of just **working hard**."

She went on to say, "Tess, I'm off by 6 pm every day except Thursday, and I am off on weekends." Chaos Awareness kicked in for me.

Melissa initiated a brand new way of thinking for me. Before my conversation with Melissa, I could not imagine closing the shop early, having weekends off, and still earning a profitable living. I took Melissa's advice and began a new career in the hair extension and hair replacement industry. It was the best thing I could have done to transform my life. Now I had a fulfilling and rewarding career helping clients with alopecia, cancer, medical hair loss, and thinning hair. It felt good enhancing the beauty and self-esteem of my clients. I no longer worked twelve or more hours a day. Finally, I had the time and energy to enjoy family, friends, and hobbies.

A few years later, I relocated my business to a larger building. I moved from a 700 square foot space to a 3,000 square foot building. I thought I was making a good decision.

Instead, I created more Chaos for myself. The location was wrong, parking was inadequate, security was nonexistent, and the rent escalated. Eventually, I lost clients. Somehow I'd created Chaos all over again. Now, in hindsight, I recognize that *I was in a state of Chaos Awareness*. Again, I want to ask, have you been in similar situations or know of someone who has?

To sum it up, I'm the girl that had it, lost it, and had it again. Remember I told you that you are the architect of your life. Now I am telling you that you get to choose your life. I did it, and I know you can do it as well. I did it by using my experiences to create *The 3 C's System*. I quickly rebounded and will show you how you can rebound, too. Let's begin with Chaos.

5 Tips to Identify the Chaos in Your Life

First, let's define Chaos as a state of disarray, confusion, and disorder, where everything is spinning out of control. As I talk to business owners, soon-to-be business owners, clients, friends, mentors, teachers, or students, I find that Chaos is present in everyone's life.

Did you recognize the states of Chaos in my story? Has Chaos shown up in your life over and over again? Let me help you to identify the Chaos in your life. It typically shows up in the following forms:

1. Anxiety: an unpleasant feeling of uneasiness accompanied by distress with feelings of ruination.

2. Worry: thoughts, images, and emotions of negativity, which churn in your mind without a positive solution.

3. Fear: the real or imagined perception of danger.

4. Doubt: a mood swing of belief and disbelief.

5. Emotion: a state of consciousness with an array of feelings ranging from frustration, sorrow, guilt, anger, pity, and envy to joy, love, and excitement.

Did that help? Can you now see where Chaos is in your life? If so, great! Remember, Chaos Awareness is the first step, and as I mentioned, most people are in or have been in a state of Chaos. That being said, it's always better to prevent Chaos, and here are some steps to doing just that.

5 Steps to Prevent Chaos in Your Life

1.) Be prepared: Preparation is the key to avoiding Chaos in your life! Preparation can include research, planning, and training. Here are a few examples.

Jane

My coaching client, Jane, had a speaking engagement at a seminar due to start in two hours. Even while driving down a busy freeway in bumper-to-bumper traffic, Jane knew she had plenty of time to arrive at the seminar, meet the organizers, and even review her notes before speaking. She always liked to arrive early to meet with participants at the invitational seminars. Suddenly she heard a loud bang and had a difficult time steering her car. She knew she had a blowout and carefully maneuvered her car to the shoulder lane. Once she came to a complete stop, she reached in her purse for her cell phone to call for roadside assistance.

She pulled everything out of her purse and even emptied it on the passenger side seat. There was no cell phone in her purse. That alone could send someone into a panic. But Jane was prepared. Her husband had taught her how to change the oil, change the windshield wipers, what to do if she heard strange sounds from her car, and yes, how to change a tire. Jane often joked with her husband, saying she'd never need to do any of those things—after all, the phone number for roadside assistance was programmed into her cell phone.

After taking a few deep breaths, Jane changed from her high-heeled shoes to flats, took off her suit jacket, went to her trunk, took out the spare tire and tire jack, and proceeded to change her tire. She heard a few car honks on that busy day, but not even the wrecker drivers stopped to assist her. Some forty minutes later, she was on her way to the speaking engagement. She made a quick stop in the ladies' room to wash her hands, touch up her makeup, and regain her composure before she confidently entered the seminar. And she wasn't late. Thanks to her preparedness, Jane avoided a chaotic situation.

Cathy

Cathy is a busy hair stylist in an urban salon. Over the years, she has developed a loyal client base. Some of her customers travel long distances from other cities for Cathy's magic touch on their hair. Cathy has a daily schedule, with appointments nearly every hour. There are days when she is so busy she cannot even take a break for lunch. She loves her work so much that the hours seem to slip away.

One day, as she was styling a new client, Cathy was distracted with a conversation in her salon and accidentally cut her hand with shears. It could have been disastrous, but quick-thinking as she was, Cathy excused herself from the room without disclosing her reason and headed to her utility closet where she kept her first aid kit. Quickly she bandaged her finger and calmly resumed the client's haircut. The new client became a recurring customer who has referred more clients to Cathy. Without preparation, Cathy would have created a chaotic scene, lost a brand new client, and even additional future clients.

Susan

Susan, an executive with her company, always reads and researches agenda topics covered in her company's monthly meetings. One morning, thirty minutes before the start of a meeting, Susan's boss surprisingly stuck his head in her office door and shouted, "Susan, Maria's not in today! Her daughter is sick. I need you to conduct today's meeting!" Susan didn't panic. She was already prepared to facilitate discussions on each agenda item. She impressed her boss that day and at subsequent meetings. Her preparedness was rewarded with additional responsibilities, a raise, and a promotion.

2.) **Be willing:** Be willing to work effectively, change in the face of adversity, and even to admit defeat. Stretch your limits by being willing to do the thing that makes you uncomfortable. Notice your thinking, and be willing to get uncomfortable to accomplish your goals.

Larry

Larry was a serious athlete who worked hours and hours perfecting his basketball techniques. He was determined to be a starter on his high school team. He thought he had an easy shot being one of the best players at his school. During practice sessions, his coaches would often ask him to try different methods and work with other players to improve his techniques. But Larry wouldn't listen. He thought he had already mastered key techniques, like cross over dribbling, back passing, turnover jumps, and three-pointers. When it came time for the team tryouts, Larry was confident and cocky. He was also rude, disrespectful, and unable to take criticism.

When the coaches posted the names of the starting players in the locker room, Larry discovered he wasn't on the list. He knew he had better technique than more than a few players on that list. Confused, he stormed out of the gym. For a few days, he sulked in disbelief. After the weekend, he gained courage and visited the head coach's office before his first class. Larry humbly asked the coach why he had not been chosen as part of the starting lineup. His coach told him he had a bad attitude and was not a team player.

Larry was crushed, but he really wanted to play basketball. He begged his coach to give him another chance. His coach allowed him to be an alternate player. So, Larry practiced with the team every day. He cooperated with his team members and with the coach. He never gave up on his dream to become a starter on the team.

Mid-season, a team member became ineligible to play against opposing teams. Larry was then called off the bench.

Do you recognize a Larry in your life? A know-it-all with a bad attitude? Do you see how your personality can influence other people? Perhaps it's your attitude that's in the way of opportunity. Notice your attitude. Be willing to change.

3.) Be cautious: Being an entrepreneur can sometimes involve risk taking—and being successful is sometimes about being careful not to risk all your accomplishments. There are some steps you can take to lessen the risk, like starting small, having a business and marketing plan, and waiting until the right opportunity is present.

Ken

Ken was a building contractor who had a business purchasing, leasing, and remodeling homes. Ken made a calculated risk to use some of his real estate as collateral to build a large luxury home. Unforeseen circumstances in the housing industry caused property values to plummet, and Ken could not even sell the luxury home or any of his other properties. The bank foreclosed on his real estate collateral. Ken was stuck with only one asset in his portfolio—the luxury home. That property drained his resources. He still had to pay property taxes, yard maintenance fees, homeowner's association fees, and utility bills.

Ken thought he had a good marketing plan by listing the property with multiple real estate agents. Realtor after realtor paraded potential buyers in the glamorous home through private showings and open houses. Months later, Ken was at his wit's end. He did not have a buyer, and he simply could not continue to maintain the home. Lowering the sales price one more time was not an option.

For more than a year, in hopes of securing a buyer, Ken talked about selling the home to everyone he met, except one close family member. Ken had no idea his family member was even in the market to buy a home. In a casual conversation at a family event, Ken spoke up and talked about the beautiful home he was trying to sell. In a matter of days, the property was sold to Ken's family member, who paid the original selling price. Today, Ken is still an entrepreneur in a different line of work. He is still taking risks—albeit smaller ones.

Ken took a big risk and nearly lost it all. Do you take risks in life? Are the risks business or personal? Would it be worth it to take a risk for a huge dividend if it meant you could lose it all? If you lost it all, could you rebound and start all over again?

Mary

Mary grew tired of commuting to a large downtown communications firm. While she was successful at her job, she felt stagnated, not being able to project her creativity. She yearned to promote small- and medium-sized businesses in local and regional media outlets. Mary was a people person at the firm. While at the communications firm, she worked with her peers to develop strategies for product placement to expand and grow some of the cities' largest companies. She never had an opportunity to work directly with business owners.

Mary had a dream to start her own marketing firm. She did her research. She attended small business

THE 3 C'S SYSTEM

luncheons, wrote articles for several local newspapers, joined professional organizations, and attended educational seminars to enhance her skills. She became an expert in her field. By the time her firm downsized, Mary already had a business plan for her own company. She knew the perfect location to open her office. She knew her potential clientele and how she would attract new business, knew how many people she needed to hire, knew the type of equipment to purchase, and had a preliminary budget in mind. All she needed was funding, and just in case she couldn't get a bank loan, she was prepared to tap into savings she had been putting aside to start her new venture.

Today, Mary is called boss at her boutique firm, where she is in charge of enhancing small businesses with creative, careful, and thoughtful marketing and advertising. Mary took risks with a plan, and as a result she is living her dream.

4.) Be methodical: Have a plan and stick to it. Know your plan, know it well, and persevere. Stick to your word. Stay focused on your goals.

Nancy

Nancy wanted to become the Chief Financial Officer at her company. She had moved up the ranks with several promotions, had years of experience, and knew she was ready for the challenge. The present CFO at her company was about to retire, and she wanted to be his replacement. Although she was highly qualified, it would not be easy to convince board members she was the right woman for the job. No other woman had held that high a position at the company.

Nancy created a vision board. First, she purchased a big white poster board from a national craft store. Then she read and scanned magazines for pictures and words to form affirmations. She then pasted the pictures and words on the poster board to paint a picture of what her life would look like as the CFO of the company. She didn't stop with the vision board. She used her cell phone to record her voice. On the recording, Nancy described in detail the responsibilities, relationships, and goals she would have in the CFO position. She also explained on her recording why she was the best candidate for the job and the talents she would bring to the company. Nancy listened to her recording daily as she traveled to work. Nancy also placed notes of positive affirmations all over the house. She stared for hours at her vision board and imagined her life as CFO.

In addition to this, she created a gratitude journal and acknowledged daily on her long list all that she appreciated. Nancy refused to consider failure in her quest to become CFO. She infused her conscious thoughts into her subconscious mind. She could feel herself in the CFO position, see it, and taste it. Today, she is CFO of that company.

Have a thought of your future and visualize it. Use your imagination and methodically make it a reality.

Cassandra

Cassandra was a bright student in school, always near the top of her class academically. She always wanted to help somebody. Often she volunteered to help her teacher pass out class assignments. If she saw a friend in need of help, there she was assisting. Cassandra was also shy, quiet, and reserved. Rarely did she express any opinions. She never wanted to cause problems for anybody.

One day, she overheard her parents talk about how bankers made a lot of money. She made a decision at the age of fifteen that she wanted to work at a bank. Her college major was accounting. But she struggled with all her business courses, making C's and D's.

She graduated from college, just barely, with a low GPA. Then she tried to find a job in the banking industry. It took her an entire year to land a position as a part-time bank teller. And once she landed that job, she hated it. Deep down, she always wanted to try a different career. During her off days, she began to volunteer. She tried substitute teaching, receptionist work, photography, and hospital volunteering. The hospital is where she felt a sense of belonging. So she enrolled in a part-time program to earn a nursing degree. After a semester, she enrolled full-time. Her grades were A's and B's. She is still in nursing school today, and she continues to volunteer at a local hospital. She used the method of volunteering to find her calling as a nurse.

Carol

Carol became a licensed beautician at the age of eighteen. While in high school, she attended a technical school. Upon graduation, she went from styling hair on her mother's front porch to owning a salon on one of the busiest streets in her city. She continued her education and methodically learned every new technique, even attending hair shows across the country and participating in style competitions. She found her favorite styling method to be non-surgical hair replacement for women. She wanted to specialize in the technique but was afraid. So she continued to say yes to every client who called her or walked into her shop. For twenty-six years, she worked 12- to 15-hour days. She had a lot of clients and no free time. On her off days, she often spent the day at the mall, buying clothes, shoes, handbags, and hats. She didn't save money and found herself living day to day and month to month, making money, paying bills, and buying more stuff. She was on a roller coaster with no direction. She knew it and often thought, *If only I could specialize in hair restoration.* But she was afraid and worried about everything. Her friends started calling her a "worrywart." Carol worried about how she would pay her property taxes, how she would repair the air conditioner in her salon, and would she still be in business next year.

One day, a client sitting in her salon gave her an idea, suggesting that Carol delegate some of her responsibilities by hiring newly licensed stylists so she could specialize in hair replacement techniques. Carol and her client methodically developed a plan. Six months later, Carol still has some of the same clients who have come in for the last twenty-six years, and she has started to accept clients in need of hair replacement. She has a newly licensed stylist, whom she supervises and her clients like. She is not worrying about her property taxes, air conditioner, or if she will be in business next year. She embraced change by thinking in a new way. She identified the Chaos in her life, became clear on her plan of action, and committed to change.

5.) Be ready: Finally, be ready! In the game of life, timing really IS everything, and if you're not ready to succeed, you simply won't. Don't get me wrong: readiness is not the same as an age, an income level, or a degree. You'll know it when you're ready because you'll feel it deep inside.

Emma

Emma worked at a busy daycare. She was a preschool teacher who truly loved working with children. But she wasn't happy with the school. She saw how the owner cut corners by not providing the children with stimulating activities. She observed how the owner was only concerned with his financial profit. Emma wanted to make a real impact on educating the children. She had a dream her students would grow up becoming happy, compassionate, and fulfilled.

As Emma continued to work at the daycare, she became increasingly unhappy. Although she continued to smile and keep a happy face, it became unbearable, and she could no longer work in misery. She gave her two-week resignation letter to her employer and began to count the days until her departure. She remained cheerful and outgoing with the students and parents. One of the parents, who had heard of Emma's resignation, approached Emma and offered her a private tutoring position for her four-year-old daughter. It was a full-time position teaching spelling, writing, numbers, art, manners, songs, and games. Emma could hardly believe her new job offer. She was thrilled and ready for the opportunity. Emma landed her dream job. She is now teaching a smart, articulate, and confident five-year-old and developing a curriculum for a preschool she plans to open in the near future. Emma can see the school, the decorations of each classroom, the teachers, and the students. She imagines her school will be the best in the city with a waiting list.

Can you see your dreams unfolding? Do you imagine your future?

Parting Words about Chaos

After years of bad decisions, Chaos Awareness drove me to take the necessary steps to gain control over my life. I made a decision to get out of my rut and get out of my own way.

You can do it, too. Stop relying on man and condition and totally rely on the higher source. Ultimately, I had no one else to blame, but I had the fear of failing like my father did, which was the root of my Chaos: fear of failure, fear of looking bad, fear of losing my income, and fear of not achieving my goals. Does this sound familiar, or do you know of someone who can identify with this? Do you know what's at the root of your Chaos? Do you know why your life feels out of control?

Now I'm going to offer you a few tips to help you manage your way to a better life by showing you how I took steps to change my business and ultimately turn my life from Chaos to Clarity.

The Chaos Awareness Questionnaire

Before we leave Chaos completely in the rearview mirror, I'd like to ask you a few questions first. Or, more specifically, I'd like to suggest that you ask yourself some questions first.

These questions will help you put guardrails around your Chaos, realize what kind of Chaos you're experiencing at the moment, and better prepare you for the benefits to come in the next two sections, **Clarity Awareness** and **Commitment Awareness** [answer them in the blanks I've provided below]:

- **What exactly is making your life so chaotic at the moment?**

  _____
  _____
  _____
  _____

- **On a scale of 1 to 10, "10" being the highest level of Chaos and "1" being the lowest, how would you rate your current state of Chaos?**

  _____
  _____
  _____
  _____

- How did reading my story of Chaos Awareness make you feel?

  _____
  _____
  _____
  _____

- How does your own sense—or state—of Chaos make you feel?

  _____
  _____
  _____
  _____

- What have you done to manage or control your Chaos?

  _____
  _____
  _____
  _____

Chapter 2
Clarity Awareness

What happened, specifically, to make me realize I needed to make a change in my life? The reason isn't difficult or challenging; it's because Chaos was repeatedly showing up in my life, leading me to Clarity Awareness. I was getting really tired of it, but more than that, I knew that if I didn't make some changes, Chaos would always be a part of my life. I just couldn't live like that anymore. This is a perfect example of Clarity Awareness.

What's worse, I would find myself attracting fear, worry, and stress due to my negative thoughts. I was basing my situation and decision-making skills on man and condition and not the higher source. Can you relate to this or know someone who can identify with this?

For example, my business decreased due to the change in the economy, and when fewer and fewer clientele started coming in, I took that personally. In my head, anyway, that became a negative reflection on me, on my work ethic, my business decisions, and I was suddenly in a state of panic. This was my old friend Chaos creeping back in. Then I made a decision to pay attention to my thought and word processing, to notice what I was not noticing: positive or negative.

It's simply called Clarity Awareness. I also began to get more careful in regards to who I let into my personal space. Not only did I try to get rid of my own "stinking thinking," but I also tried to reduce the amount of "downer people" in my life. I saw what had been happening in my life for so long, in a new light. I could even become grateful for the obstacles that I was experiencing, because I was gaining wisdom from it all.

There are several people who inspired me to overcome the Chaos that was consuming me during this period and find more Clarity in my life. The first is Sara Blakey, founder of Spanx. The hosiery company, now worth an estimated $150 million, came about when Sara stopped selling fax machines and created a homemade solution to an everyday problem women have. By cutting the feet off her pantyhose to help women look better in their clothes, Sara created Spanx, a multimillion-dollar international apparel company.

Sara started with $5,000, which she'd earned from selling fax machines. She could have gone on selling fax machines forever, but Sara had an entrepreneurial vision. She became a millionaire several times over. More than that, **she owns 100 percent of the company**. Sara took an idea of her own and made it big. And it all started because she didn't like the way her butt looked in her white pants! So what did she do? Simple: she cut the foot out of the pantyhose!

This is something that I have done myself for years, but Sara reinvented it and created footless pantyhose that wouldn't roll up, and could do well under pants, skirts, and dresses. Her idea and her persistence saw her through.

Sara had never taken a business class and had never worked in the fashion or retail industry. She had simply been visualizing a different life for herself for years and wanted to create her first million at thirty years of age—and she did.

She is truly an inspiration to me. Sara is an example of Clarity Awareness.

Another personal inspiration for me is J.K. Rowling, author of the wildly successful *Harry Potter* children's book series. Rowling suffered dozens of rejections when trying to get the books published, but she persisted. Today, she is one of the wealthiest women in Britain.

Steve Stoute is an author, entrepreneur, advertising executive, and an American record executive and artist manager. He is also a huge inspiration for me. Steve has liberated brands from cultural stereotypes through his creative strategies. He is the CEO, Founder, and Managing Director of Carol's Daughter, which is an African American natural hair care line and body product.

Steve is also the author of *The Tanning of America*, or how hip-hop created different rules of the new economy. These are just some of the things that Steve Stoute has co-founded and created in his stellar and inspirational career. He is truly amazing, and has inspired me to the highest power. Steve's story is another example of Clarity Awareness.

Bethenny Frankel is an author, entrepreneur, TV personality, and natural food cook. She went from delivering pastries out of her car to becoming a multi-millionaire. She has appeared on *The Martha Stewart Show*, *The Apprentice*, and *The Real Housewives of New York*. Founder of Skinnygirl, Frankel sold her Skinnygirl brand to Fortune Brands' Beam Global for an estimated $120 million dollars. Bethenny's strong work ethic and determination are an inspiration to me, and she truly exemplifies *The 3 C's System*.

What all four of these brilliant, amazing, and inspiring people had in common was one driving force: Clarity of Vision.

They knew exactly what they wanted, and that Clarity helped them create goal and action plans for just how to get it.

Susan

Susan, a coaching client, knew when Clarity Awareness made a huge difference in her life. Susan had a property tax issue, and she was past due several years due to divorce and a reduction in income. She is a senior citizen who had uncontrolled negative thoughts her entire life. Then Susan started using *The 3 C's System* and everything changed: she received an increase in pay on her job, then she received unexpected family funds from the sale of family property—and this unexpected income allowed Susan to pay her property tax. Can you relate to this situation, or do you know someone who can identify with this?

5 Tips on Achieving Clarity Awareness

So, enough about letting others inspire you; now it's time to inspire yourself. To do just that, I'm now going to offer you **five simple tips** to help you manage your way to a better life by showing you how I took steps to change my business/career and, ultimately, my life.

Tip #1: *Decision*

Make up your mind to live and have what you want. Stop being indecisive and stay stern.

Becky

Becky is a seventy-five-year-old divorcee, who six years ago left a six-figure income as a social worker and her part-time job at a local hospital admitting patients who had mental issues. Becky was unhappy in her marriage and decided, after marrying the same man twice, that it wasn't going to work. Becky was living in an apartment, and her family members suggested that she live in a senior's facility, but Becky didn't want that; she wanted a home of her own. As a result, Becky made a decision for herself that within ninety days, she would purchase a new home, while earning less money but gaining peace of mind. She gave it all up: fine clothes, furniture, houses, and income to move to another state and live off her retirement. Becky made a decision and started over. This is what a made up mind will do. Does this sound familiar, or do you know someone who can relate?

When you make a decision to do something, everything shows up for it to manifest.

Tip # 2: *Budget Your Money Wisely*
I'm not one to necessarily say that money is the root of ALL evil, but as one who has had money, lost it, and earned it back, I can say that few life issues are as stressful as the lack of money. To avoid adding this one issue to your life, you need to budget your money more wisely.

Budgeting helps ease your mind about money. When you know clearly and concisely what you want to accomplish, financially speaking, you can work with that. Here's how to make, and stick to, a budget:

- **Put together a monthly spending plan.** Buy a calendar or use computer software to help you keep track of how much money you make, how you spend it, and where you spend it. Today, many banks will provide you with an electronic statement that can help you do just that. If yours doesn't, switch banks!

- **Keep an income journal.** Writing down what you make every week, and how you spend it, will also force you to keep track of what you're spending your money on. Write in your journal every time you receive and spend money; this will make you more conscious of your spending when you see it on paper. This can be a hard habit to start, but an even harder habit to break—a good thing! I still write down everything I spend, and it helps me to really think twice about what I spend my money on and how often.

- **Set a goal.** Goals are critical because they provide starting lines, finish lines, stop signs, and even guardrails for what you hope to achieve. Make a decision, and then be clear regarding what you want for your finances. This is a call for Clarity Awareness. When you have a specific goal in mind, like saving up for the down payment on your new business or on new office space, you're less likely to go "off budget" and waste your money on mindless, random things.

- **Sacrifice.** Sometimes, you have to give up a few things now, so you can have peace, joy, and happiness later. For example, let's say you set a simple, short-term goal that says, "I'm going to stop buying my coffee at a café on the way to work every morning this week and put the $37 dollars I'd save directly into my savings account." Sure, NOT splurging on your favorite double espresso whipped hurts a little, but when you think of how much you spend just to indulge yourself every day, then compare it with how quickly that money could add up to something like a new computer, down payment, class, or seminar, you're clearly seeing how sacrificing a little now pays off BIG later.

When I first learned how to budget, I began to make changes in my physical space. I actually moved to a smaller location and cut my living expenses, both personally and professionally. This was a difficult decision because I had to cut my losses. At the time, it hurt a lot. Today, I realize sometimes we have to take steps back in order to move forward.

Tip # 3: *Meditate Regularly*
When it comes to daily, or at least regular habits, few things help bring Clarity more into focus than meditation. Think of how much you might get accomplished, or at least see more clearly, if you could take 10, 15, 20, or even 30 minutes out of each day/week to meditate, focus, and find Clarity.

The purpose of meditation is to get positive energy flowing and to increase your power of manifestation. What is manifestation? It's visualizing the life you want before turning that vision into a spiritual and physical reality. Your thought process helps you to create the life you want. When you have a peaceful mind, you have the ability to create great ideas that flow into reality. Since I began meditating regularly, I am no longer living in Chaos; I have Clarity in my life. I watch my spoken words, and I've learned that, good or bad, my thought process is the key to how I live my life, day in and day out.

Since I've started meditating, I am also reading spiritual and self-help books daily. Every day I list three or more things for which I am grateful. My life has changed for the highest good, and it's truly amazing.

Seeking and finding clarity has helped revolutionize how I live my life and how I do business. My sister and I have created a wig and hair extension line that looks natural and feels great for the woman who has thinning hair, medical hair loss, alopecia, or cancer. Stay tuned for the launch! I am also an educator, cosmetologist, author, speaker, and transformational coach all because I sought Clarity.

Personally, I am more relaxed, happier, and find that now things just flow. If you would like to find more Clarity in your life through meditation, here are some simple steps to follow:

1. When meditating, select a quiet place at a comfortable temperature for you.

2. Ensure that you have enough time to meditate thoroughly. Thirty minutes is usually my goal or desired time for meditation.

3. You may find that soft music, or nature's sounds, help you enter a meditative state—or you may need pure silence.

4. Relax and put your mind at ease. Don't let negative or unproductive thoughts enter your head.

5. Focus on the positive energy that meditation creates. Don't use the time to schedule, categorize, plot,

or plan. Use it to sit quietly and open yourself to the world around you.

6. Meditate daily, if possible, and for at least three times per week.

Tip # 4: *Lead a More Balanced Life*

- Work less and work smart by delegating to a staff member

- Take a lunch break and stop working through lunch

- Stop letting others dictate your time, and work on a schedule

- Enjoy time with your family, and take yearly vacations

Creating a balanced life means having great health, love, spirituality, family, understanding, and direction in your life. It means sensing when things are slipping out of balance and into Chaos. It doesn't mean leading a perfect life, by any means, but balance means that no one area of your life ever gets too out of control.

We will always experience unavoidable times where emergencies happen, like a check that bounces or a sick child or a flat tire or more clients than we can handle. The more balance we have in the other areas of our lives, the more energy and creativity we'll have when we're trying to handle these occasional, unavoidable flare ups and emergencies.

When you get rid of the negative thoughts, which create imbalance, you are able to come up with ideas you may not have considered. Because I worked hard to maintain balance in my life, I am now able to create what I want for my life by using my true talent, which is creating products and services that will help women look and feel beautiful again. Tuning in to myself through meditation has helped me to create my Transformational Coaching programs and will create my future online custom wig and hair extension line.

What's more, balance is the opposite of Chaos. Chaos is when everything in your life is out of balance, when every emotion seems extreme, and when every minor issue becomes a disaster. When your life is so out of balance, your emotions are frayed and you can't see things clearly. Balance helps you look at the world objectively, and brings Clarity to all that you do.

Chapter 3
Commitment Awareness

You can't change the **Chaos** in your life, or keep the **Clarity**, if you're not **Committed** to your own personal and professional success. Being committed means making a pledge or becoming dedicated to a goal, or promise, that you will stay the course regardless of obstacles. This *Third C*, **Commitment**, requires dedication, vision, and purpose and is essential for all entrepreneurs!

10 Tips to Help You Stay Committed to Your Goals

I was determined to create a very specific lifestyle for myself, one where I could be independent, work smart AND hard, and achieve my very individual goals.

I was committed to my goals of having my own wig line, an extension line, as well as being an author and coach to others. Obviously, the more ambitious your goals are, the more Committed you have to be. There was no way I could reach all of my goals without having very specific goals and guidelines for myself every step of the way. This is an example of Commitment.

Athiea

Athiea was a freshman in college when her mother became ill and needed lifesaving surgery. While her mother was in the hospital, her father threatened to leave her mother. Athiea's home life was chaotic. When her mother was discharged from the hospital, she was unable to care for herself and needed round-the-clock care. Family members had to step in to assist because Athiea's father left and never returned. Her mother went on welfare, and Athiea wanted to quit school to help her family, but her stern grandmother encouraged her to hang in there and not quit college. This is when Athiea realized she was in a Chaos Awareness state.

Athiea was determined to keep striving toward a better future even if she was broke and sad. She then began reading books and listening to tapes about positive thinking, and this awoke her to Clarity Awareness. Now she knew exactly what she wanted in life. Her circumstances caused her to realize that adversity is temporary, and when you are faced with adversity head on, you get closer to your goals. Adversity also builds something inside of you— character. It helps you to determine what you really want for your life. Athiea knew that if she wasn't clear on what she wanted, she wouldn't get it. Athiea was now at the Clarity Awareness state of her life.

Through Commitment and Commitment Awareness, Athei completed her college education and is now the caregiver for her mother. Athiea used *the 3 C's System* to help her overcome her circumstances. Can you identify with Athiea's story, or do you know someone who can? Are you ready to create Commitment in your life? Read on for my 10 tips to help you stay committed to your goals.

1.) Be goal oriented: As part of my Commitment plan, I set daily goals and priorities in each area of my life to help achieve my new life of abundance. I made sure that every single day, I Committed a certain amount of time, energy, and progress to each goal.

2.) Be disciplined: I am disciplined, and I mean *very* disciplined; my goals are non-negotiable. I am not willing to allow anything to get in my way of Commitment to my goals. If it is time to work on my wig line, I make the time for it. If I am going to set aside two hours a day to write, I keep that schedule, whether I find 15 minutes at lunch, 30 minutes after my shop closes, and another hour and 15 minutes before bed.

3.) Create a vision board: I created a vision board, and it is the first thing I look at in the morning and the last thing I look at before retiring for the evening. On this board are pictures or drawings or magazine cut-outs of the things I want to achieve in life: an award or a bestselling book or a woman speaking to a crowd of thousands and a brand new salon. My board is full of the things I want for myself, and not just material possessions but also accomplishments I want to achieve. I can't tell you how important it is for me to see this board first thing every morning. It really helps me stay Committed to my goals.

4.) Plan your work, work your plan: I set a plan each week and follow it daily. Each day I meditate and participate in the spiritual reading of self-help books and affirmations. I have set boundaries for myself, and my time. I knew I needed to accomplish certain things each day in order to complete my goals.

5.) Put it in writing: One way to assure that you are Committed is to actually write down your plan for the day. With our hectic schedules, it is easy to let the day get away from us. Emails, text messaging, commuting to work, cooking for a family, and keeping a smooth running home are all important, but we can't forget the Commitment to our own needs, and our own dreams and goals. Writing your goals keeps you focused.

6.) Keep a schedule: Making a schedule helps you keep track of time, manage it better, and utilize your time more effectively. Even if it's just a "to be" list. When you can see and feel the END in mind, you can accomplish anything you want for your life. Scheduling helps you prioritize the tasks you need to accomplish.

7.) Monitor your thoughts: Thoughts are very important toward keeping you committed. You must think a certain way, and that way is **positive**! Being positive means noticing what you are thinking every moment of the day. The moment you starting doubting yourself you must change your thinking.

8.) Stay positive: Keeping a positive attitude helps you attract positive things in your life. Be Committed within your boundaries, and have the ability to collaborate with others who share your vision and who can help you achieve your goals. Change your thoughts if you start thinking negative.

9.) Create a team: You can't do it alone. Find like-minded people to help you achieve your goals and share in your success. Be accountable, either to yourself or someone else, and do whatever it takes to achieve your goal. Network with others and help others during this process. No one succeeds alone. We all need someone else to help us grow, and we can help them grow, too. If you're succeeding just to succeed, what's the point in that? I take great joy in helping others in my line of work; it's in my job description!

10.) Continuously challenge yourself: When you reach one goal, pat yourself on the back, have a snack, take a break, celebrate...then get right back to work! There is no such thing as a plateau in success; there is always another mountain, hill, or obstacle to climb. And that's okay; that's part of the great journey of success!

Parting Words about Commitment Awareness
What You Think About, You Bring About

Successful people **think a certain way**. Some are born thinking this way while others ease into it, like I did. Successful people are wired to think in successful terms. They set a goal and work with the end in mind. Success first starts with thoughts and then manifestation through creation. It's amazing, and I've seen it happen in real life.

You can visualize your success, but just thinking it isn't enough. Successful people put their thoughts into action. My vision board would have been just a pretty decoration if I didn't stay Committed to my goals and purposefully achieve them, day in and day out. That's what Commitment is all about, first imagining success, then creating it in the real world. Maintaining continuous success is all about staying balanced with what you desire by keeping positive thoughts a priority. In other words: **what you think about, you bring about.**

If you choose to think negative thoughts, you *will* attract negativity in your life. For example, when my clientele decreased, I stayed the course rather than blaming others or giving up. I started visualizing new clients daily in my business and kept reminding myself that I am not relying on man and condition, but that I am totally relying on a higher source.

Every day I choose three different things for which I am grateful, and like magic, my dreams manifest. Being grateful allows more things to unfold in my life, things I cannot even imagine. I am more creative and energetic so I can educate other cosmetologists about hair restoration.

I work in an industry I love, doing what I love, coaching and educating. I know I control my thoughts in every moment, and that makes a huge difference in the outcomes I create. The wisdom I have learned is that all obstacles that have come my way are a test.

I have passed the test!

And now, thanks to *The 3 C's System*, so can you!

Conclusion

So there you have it. *The 3 C's System* is the ultimate help guide to motivate you toward success.

1.) Chaos Awareness: Don't be afraid to look at your current state of Chaos and use it as a "diving board" into a life filled with Clarity and Commitment.

2.) Clarity Awareness: Be clear about what you want, set your goals, communicate them often, write them down, and focus on the future, not the past.

3.) Commitment Awareness: Be committed to making your dream a reality through daily, righteous, and purposeful action(s).

I hope this book inspires you to put *The 3 C's System* into action in the way that works best for you. My personal wish is that you enjoy embracing *The 3C's System* as much as I did. Implementing this system and following your heart will propel you to an amazing life!

Don't worry if the stories you have read are not exactly like yours. It's up to you to use *The 3 C's System* to personalize and propel your own success! I share my story to show you how well this worked for me, and how discovering *The C's* is half the battle.

Now it's your turn to write your own story!

Acknowledgments

To everyone who has been an inspiration in my life, so I could help others transform their lives forever, I sincerely THANK YOU.

First, I thank God for my gifts and talents, which allow me to give back to the world.

To my mom and dad for giving me life. Dad, thanks for showing me a great work ethic, and Mom, thanks for being my biggest fan. I love you both.

To my daughter Porsha, who is so talented. Thanks for being supportive when it counts.

To my sister Sonia—oh my gosh! Amazing! Amazing! Thanks for being a big sister even though you are the younger one.

To my other siblings—Cedric, Eric, Kendall, and Verna (Brenda)—thank you all for having a listening ear when I need it.

To my clients and students, I say thank you all for having faith in my talent to service you.

To my friend Melissa English, who gave me a word of encouragement in how to enjoy life and work smart.

To my special friends, Connie Lyons and Veronica Love, thanks for being there through it all. And I cherish all my other friends. You know who you are.

To Joan Jefferson and JoAnne Barnes, I want to say thank you guys for introducing me to a new way of thinking years ago. You are all an inspiration to me. I am forever grateful for your support.

To Christal Jackson, I want to especially thank you for giving me the encouragement to write. Thank you so much.

To Jennifer Ashby from Consciously Created, your support in helping me to connect with my authentic voice and unique gifts, and then communicate this with the world, has made all the difference. From my branding, to website, to anything I needed, your talent and commitment shines bright. I don't know what I would have done without you!

To Peggy McColl, Mary Morrissey, Bob Proctor, and Gay Henderick, I say thanks for your extraordinary coaching, which caused the shift in my thinking. Peggy McColl, through your coaching, you made me more creative than I have ever been in my life, and thank you for being so understanding when it counts. I am so grateful and thank you guys very much.

To my team— my nephew Eric Anderson and David Johnson, amazing young men with a great gift in Social Media and Graphic Arts, and my virtual assistant, LuAnne Hage from Virtual Relief, who partners with me to develop and implement the products and programs from my dreams to reality.

To everyone else in my life, I'm so thankful and grateful.

Finally, to those of you whom I have yet to have the pleasure of meeting, thanks for being interested in the message of *The 3 C's System* to achieve success. I am so grateful for the opportunity to be your coach and speaker. Thanks again.

Are you ready to work with Tess and see real results in your life?

Reach out to schedule your FREE Strategy Session with me, and let's determine how I can best serve you. It's time to create the results you desire, and I am here to support you every step of the way!

I want you to know that you can create anything (yes, anything) you desire in life, and I can show you how. We all have our stories, challenges, and issues... everyone. And we can all make the choice to change.

- Have you realized that your thoughts are always negative, but you are not sure how to stop them?

- Have you found yourself doing, doing, and doing even more for everyone else first, and would like some support identifying your true worth?

- Do you keep attracting the same types of negative relationships and situations in your life and are ready to change the cycle?

- Would you like to remove the barriers and blocks that prevent you from creating the life you know you desire and deserve?

- Do you simply want more out of your life?

Simply put, life is a series of CHOICES. The quality of your life will, in a very big way, always reflect the quality of the choices you make. I wrote this book to help you make better choices and create a BETTER LIFE. *The 3 C's System* is the story of my own journey. It is a collection of strategies for achieving success, and it is a roadmap designed to guide you to successfully reaching your own destination!

Contact me TODAY at TessTims.com for your FREE 30-minute Strategy Session

And I'd love to hear your thoughts about this book! Email me here support@tesstims.com

About Tess

I AM A girl who understands struggle! I was raised in an entrepreneurial family where money wasn't an object, but there was always work to do and never enough time. At age twelve, I was working long hours at our family business, wearing $300 boots and diamond earrings. By age seventeen, I was on welfare. What happened? Well, I became pregnant and my father disowned me as if I had committed murder. I was left homeless with no money, no clothes, and no car. I had to get on welfare in order to support my daughter.

Four weeks after my daughter's birth, I marched down to the Department of Human Services and stated, "I don't want welfare anymore. I am getting a job, and I am going to college to provide a better life for me and my daughter." I enrolled in college. It took me six years to receive a four-year bachelor's degree, but I stuck with it. I kept the course. I reminded myself everyday where I came from and what I wanted to create for my life. Then, I created it!

I have struggled, and I have succeeded. I have been lost. I have searched. I have studied. I have learned. And now, here I stand, willing and ready to support you so that you don't have to go through all that I went through. What I clearly see now is that changing your life can be easy, and I can show you how.

With the experience of all my struggles and success, all my knowledge, and all my heart, I am here to support you. Reach out to schedule your FREE Strategy Session, and let's determine how I can best serve you. It's time to create the results you desire, and I am here to support you every step of the way!

I am the architect of my life. And guess what… YOU are the architect of your life. The question is, what are you creating?

www.ingramcontent.com/pod-product-compliance
Lightning Source LLC
Chambersburg PA
CBHW071818170526
45167CB00003B/1352